IT'S AMAZING!
SUPERCARS

Annabel Savery

FRANKLIN WATTS
LONDON•SYDNEY

First published in 2011 by
Franklin Watts
338 Euston Road
London NW1 3BH

Franklin Watts Australia
Level 17/207 Kent Street
Sydney NSW 2000

© 2011 Franklin Watts

A CIP catalogue record for this book is available from the British Library.

Planning and production by Discovery Books Limited
Managing editor: Laura Durman
Editor: Annabel Savery
Designer: Ian Winton

Picture credits: Corbis: p. 5 (Transtock), p. 11 (Bruce Benedict / Transtock), p. 16 (Transtock), p. 24 (Bruce Benedict / Transtock), p. 25 top (Transtock); Getty Images: p. 22 (Hugo Philpott/Stringer), p. 23 top (Fiona McLeod/Contributor); Jaguar: p. 21; Koenisegg: p. 10 (carstudio.it), p. 14 (Stuart Collins); Lamborghini: p. 15 top; Rex Features: p. 27 (Sony Pics/Everett), p. 28 (Everett Collection), p. 29 top (Erik C Pendzich); Shutterstock: title & p. 8 (Olga Besnard), p. 4 (Neil Roy Johnson), p. 7 top & p.7 bottom (Maksim Tooome), p. 9 & p. 31 (Max Earey), p. 15 bottom (Max Earey), p. 17 (Max Earey), p. 18 (DDCoral), p. 19 (Dongliu), p. 20 (Tito Wong), p. 23 bottom (Jaggat), p. 25 bottom (Anatoliy Meshkov), p. 26 (KSPhotography), p. 29 bottom (breezeart.us); www.carphoto.co.uk: p. 6, p. 12, p. 13.

Cover: Corbis (Guy Spangenberg/Transtock)

Every attempt has been made to clear copyright. Should there be any inadvertent omission, please apply to the publisher for rectification.

A CIP catalogue record for this book is available from the British Library.

Dewey Decimal Classification Number: 629.2'221

ISBN: 978 1 4451 0545 1

Franklin Watts is a division of Hachette Children's Books, an Hachette UK company.
www.hachette.co.uk
Printed in China

CONTENTS

All words in **bold** appear in the glossary on page 30.

SUPERCOOL SUPERCARS!

Supercars are the fastest, most expensive cars on the road.

They are made to be light and sleek, like this Ferrari. They have huge engines so that they can travel fast.

Supercars are really rare. They are expensive to build and buy, so car companies do not make many. For example, McLaren only made six copies of their supercar, the F1 LM model.

Road cars, not racing cars

Even though supercars can go incredibly fast, they are still made for people to drive on the roads. Racing cars, like those made for Formula 1, can only be driven on the race track.

THE DESIGN

Supercars are not designed to carry lots of people or a load of shopping. Every part is designed to make them go fast and look great!

Gull wing doors

Lots of supercars have **gull wing** or scissor doors. This means they open upwards, instead of outwards. On some cars the roof lifts up too!

Supercars are built so that they are very close to the ground. This means that only a little bit of air can pass underneath them. They also have a very **streamlined** shape so that air travels over them easily. Both of these **features** help the car to go faster.

IT'S AMAZING!
The Maserati MC12 supercar lifts up at the front so that it can go over speed bumps.

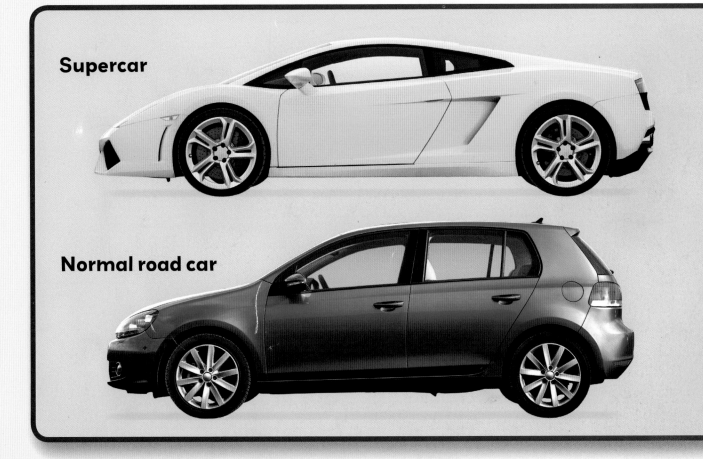

Supercar

Normal road car

KEY FEATURES

Every part of a supercar has a special function. Look at the labels to find out what each part is for.

Spoiler This helps to keep the back end of the car on the ground when travelling at high speeds.

Body This is made from a very light material, such as **carbon fibre** or **aluminium.** This means that the engine does not have to carry too much weight.

Engine The engine is very powerful. Sometimes it is in the middle of the supercar, not at the front like most road cars.

Brakes The brakes are made of special material to help the supercar brake quickly at high speed without getting too hot.

Did you know...

A car engine's power is measured in brake horse power (bhp). The average road car has between 100–200 bhp. Supercar engines often have more than 600 bhp!

TOP SPEEDS

So, how fast is fast? A normal road car's top speed would probably be less than 177 kilometres per hour (110 miles per hour).

Supercars are much faster. Some can travel at speeds above 400 kph (250 mph).

One of the best things about supercars is their **acceleration**. They can reach high speeds much quicker than normal road cars.

NOW THAT'S FAST!

The Bugatti Veyron (above) can reach 96 kph in 2.5 seconds. An average car might take between eight and ten seconds to get to that speed!

MAKING A SUPERCAR

Supercars give designers the chance to see how high-tech they can make a car.

Not many supercars are built, so they are often made one at a time. Each part is designed and crafted to be the best it can possibly be.

The picture above was taken in the Bugatti factory. Each Bugatti Veyron is put together by just eight people!

People who buy supercars can decide what they want them to look like. Buyers can choose the colour of the inside and outside of the car, and can ask for any special **gadgets** (see page 15) that they want inside it.

One of a kind

British businessman Peter Saywell wanted a Pagani Zonda Cinque, but all five had sold out. So, he **commissioned** Pagani to make one just for him. Here it is!

BEHIND THE WHEEL

The inside of a supercar is just as highly designed as the outside.

Supercars must have everything that a road car has. A gearstick, steering wheel, dials to show the speed, a **fuel gauge** and so on. But in a supercar they are much smarter.

GREAT GADGETS!

Supercars are often filled with fantastic gadgets. The Lamborghini Gallardo LP 570-4 Superleggera has a rear view camera fixed underneath the back spoiler!

Driving a supercar is a new experience for most drivers. The car is low to the ground and the fast acceleration pushes the driver back in the seat.

ON THE RACE TRACK

As speed limits on the roads are the same for every car, supercars cannot travel any faster on roads than other cars.

If supercar drivers want to test out their high-powered engines, they have to go to a race track. Race tracks are like roads in a complete loop. Here, drivers compete for the fastest lap times.

On the race track there are long, straight sections where the cars can go as fast as possible.

IT'S AMAZING!

In race track tests the Lamborghini Reventón (above) reached an average top speed of 340 kph (210 mph)!

MOTOR SHOWS

Each year, at different locations around the world, large, glamorous motor shows are held. These are the most important days of the year for car designers.

At motor shows car designers show off their latest supercars. Car **manufacturers** want to impress the visitors with the latest technology.

Many of the supercars shown at motor shows are **prototypes** like the Ferrari below. These are the first models that are made from the designs.

Inspirational cars

Motor shows are like big car fashion shows. Other car makers are inspired by the top prototype designs. They use these ideas to make simpler versions that become the road cars that everyone can buy.

ELECTRIC SUPERCARS

One of the biggest problems with cars is that they are very environmentally unfriendly. Their engines produce **exhaust fumes** that **pollute the air**.

GREEDY SUPERCARS!

Supercars have huge engines that need a lot of fuel to run. Some only travel 1.7 kilometres (1 mile) on a litre of fuel! Normal road cars travel around 11.25 kilometres (7 miles) per litre.

Exhaust pipes

Car manufacturers are working on designs to make cars better for the environment. **Hybrid** cars have been developed that run on both liquid fuel, like petrol or diesel, and electricity.

Electric supercars look just as good as other supercars, and they travel just as fast. One of the top electric supercars is the Jaguar CX75 (above).

SUPERCAR OWNERS

Supercars cost lots of money, so not many people can afford to own them. They are usually bought by people who are very rich. Some even own more than one!

Car collection

Jay Kay of pop group Jamiroquai has a big car collection. Among them are a black Ferrari Enzo and a red Lamborghini Miurathe supercar (below).

Supermodel Jodie Kidd (right) is mad about cars. She owned a Lamborghini Murcielago (right) and now has a Lamborghini Evolioné. Her other favourites are the Bugatti Veyron and the Maserati MC12.

Lewis Hamilton

Racing driver Lewis Hamilton has been promised a unique McLaren F1 LM supercar if he wins two Formula 1 championships!

SOME OF THE BEST

The Bugatti Veyron, McLaren F1 and Ferrari Enzo are fantastic supercars.

The Bugatti Veyron (above) is the most expensive supercar. It costs £1,100,000, and that's a basic model! It is also the fastest supercar. In tests it has reached 429 kph (267 mph).

The McLaren F1 LM (below) is also extremely fast. Its top speed is 389 kph (242 mph). The doors open upwards and look like a bat's wings.

The Ferrari Enzo (above) is the fourth most expensive supercar. Ferrari are so proud of this supercar that they named it after their founder – Enzo Ferrari.

SUPERCARS IN THE MOVIES

Action movies often feature stars whizzing around in powerful supercars.

Tony Stark is the man inside the Iron Man suit. In the *Iron Man* films, he drives Audi R8 cars, like the one below.

Audi R8 5.2 FSI

The Audi R8 Spyder is handmade and has lots of amazing features. It can reach 100 kph (62 mph) in 4.1 seconds, and the spoiler slides out automatically when the car goes fast!

James Bond is an impressive supercar driver. In each film he has a brand new car and he always manages to crash it!

007's supercars

Of course, James Bond doesn't have a normal supercar. His cars are kitted out with weapons, ejector seats and armour plating.

The latest films show James Bond driving an Aston Martin Vanquish or Aston Martin DBS.

FANTASY SUPERCARS

Some supercars are so amazing that they can only have come from a very creative imagination!

Batman's Batmobile is probably the coolest fantasy car there is. With rocket power and armour plating, Batman is sure to arrive safely.

A special design!

Director Steven Spielberg asked Lexus to use their latest technology to design a car (below) for the film *Minority Report*. The car was specially fitted for the film's star Tom Cruise.

Transformer Bumblebee can turn himself into a speedy yellow supercar. In the movie he becomes a Chevrolet Camaro supercar.

GLOSSARY

acceleration when a vehicle increases speed

aluminium a strong, light silver metal, which does not rust easily

armour plating very strong metal that is used to protect vehicles

carbon fibre a material that is very strong and very lightweight

commission to ask someone to make something exactly how you would like it

exhaust fumes the gas produced when an engine runs

features a part or quality of something

fuel gauge a device that tells you how much fuel is in the fuel tank

function the job that an object or gadget does

gadget a device with a clever design or unusual use

gull wing doors that have hinges at the top instead of the sides, so that they open upwards

high-tech using the latest technology

hybrid a combination of two things

manufacturers people who make or build cars

pollute to make something unclean

prototype an experimental model that is made from the first designs

streamlined a smooth shape that air can pass over easily

unique one of a kind

FURTHER INFORMATION

Books

Design It Yourself: Supercars, John Richards, Tangerine Press, 2005.

Motormania, Penny Worms, Franklin Watts, 2010.

Supercars, (Fast!), Ian Graham, QED Publishing, 2010.

Supercars, (Machine Mania), Frances Ridley, TickTock Books, 2007.

Top Gear: Best Bits: Supercars, BBC Children's Books, 2008.

Websites

Find pictures and details of all the best supercars at Supercar World.

www.supercarworld.com/cgi-bin/index.cgi

Search here for reviews and images of the top supercars.

www.supercars.net/

The website for the TV series *Top Gear*.

www.topgear.com/uk/

INDEX